TRICK OR TEA

A SHORT STORY PREQUEL TO TEA SHOP FOR TWO,
PART OF THE LOVE ON BELMONT SERIES

LORI WOLF-HEFFNER

HEAD IN THE GROUND PUBLISHING

© 2020 Lori Wolf-Heffner

All rights reserved. This book or any portion thereof may not be reproduced or used in any manner whatsoever without the express written permission of the publisher except for the use of brief quotations in a book review.

Some characters and events in this book are fictitious. Any similarity to real persons, living or dead, is coincidental and not intended by the author.

ISBN ebook: 978-1-989465-20-2

ISBN print: 978-1-989465-21-9

Editing by Susan Fish

Cover design by Fresh Design

All photographs from Shutterstock

Head in the Ground Publishing

Waterloo, Ontario, Canada

headintheground.com

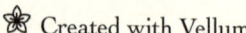 Created with Vellum

To Mom, for developing my love of herbal teas. May Claire eventually agree with you.

TRICK OR TEA—A SHORT STORY

Claire pulled her knees up to her chest and lifted her cup of Earl Claire tea to her lips as the familiar *Cheers* theme song heralded the start of a brand new episode. Earl Claire was her own blend of premium Ceylon, Darjeeling, and Assam teas, bergamot oil, vanilla, and a touch of lavender. She drank her tea whenever she felt down, which meant it had become a daily habit over the past months.

Richard entered just as the theme song ended and the show broke to commercial. Next year would be their 20th anniversary. Claire had a few wrinkles and some strands of grey to prove it while Richard had a growing bald spot. Now officially parents to two teen girls, thirteen-year-old Dawn and seven-teen-year-old Pauline, Claire and Richard's happy life was sometimes flavoured with intense drama, but the four of them laughed together a lot, too.

What was happening to Claire's Tea Shop, however, was no laughing matter.

"I can smell Earl Claire in every room," Richard said.

Only half-listening to her husband, Claire stared at the television, too discouraged to even pick up the remote and skip the commercials.

"Oh, god, no, not this one." Claire's nose wrinkled in disgust as a commercial for tea bags came on.

"Oh, pity," Richard teased. "I like that one."

But Claire's face remained serious, her tone stern. "Not funny."

Cheers returned. The new replacement for Shelley Long — Kirstie Alley as Rebecca Howe — strutted in. "Shelley Long was personable," Claire said to no one in particular. "But Kirstie is very much in charge." Claire loved seeing women in charge on television, but she preferred those with refinement, more Clair Huxtable or Angela Bower than Rebecca Howe.

"Shelley was more beautiful," Richard said, reaching over to his wife. "Like you."

Claire pulled herself away. "Not after that tea

comment. Besides, I'm too tired." She took another sip and adjusted herself in her papasan chair to face him. "I'm sorry, Richard. I've been trying so hard to keep the shop in the black these past few months—"

"No pun intended?" Richard flashed a hopeful smile, but all he got in response was tightened lips. "Sorry."

Claire hit the pause button on the remote. "I was hoping that going non-smoking would help with sales. But it's not just that."

"Tea bags."

"Tea bags. And now herbal teas—also in tea bags, I might add... If I don't make a killing—and I mean *a killing*—on Christmas sales, I'll have to close. I expected a quiet summer—that's usually the way things are—but we're now into October and nothing's picked up."

She stared at her teacup and sighed. Tea bags, herbals, and the doughnut shop down the street that still allowed smoking inside were all her competition and they were winning.

Claire tossed the remote to Richard as she got up, teacup still in hand. "I'm not going to learn anything by watching *Cheers*. Maybe the Goddess of Tea will give me an idea." The Goddess of Tea was what she called the vast collection of tea in her home office, where she also had an electric kettle. Maybe tonight would be the night she'd come up with the most incredible idea ever and save Claire's Tea Shop.

On her way to her office, she saw Dawn at the kitchen table, a teen magazine in front of her, playing with the phone cord as she talked to a friend. "I don't know, Emily," Dawn said. "Michael J. Fox is short, but I still think he's cuter than Kirk Cameron…That's true. Kirk's curls are to die for…"

As Claire passed the door to the basement, rock music seeped from underneath it. She walked downstairs to see Pauline doing push-ups in time with the music.

"Have you finished your homework?" Claire asked.

"It'll be done by morning," Pauline puffed between breaths as she pushed up. Only now did Claire notice the barbell weight on her daughter's back.

"You need good marks if you're going to go to university, Pauline."

"I know. It'll be done. I promise." She grunted as she finished her last reps. Pauline collapsed onto her stomach and removed the weight.

"And you're working at the shop tomorrow right

after school. Don't forget."

Pauline pushed herself onto her knees and adjusted the sweat band on her head. "I've got that rally tomorrow, Mom. I'm the mascot now. I have to be at every sports event. You signed the permission form, remember?"

In truth, Claire hadn't read the form in its entirety. The only thought in her mind had been that Pauline needed an outlet for her energy, otherwise she drove the family nuts. In a loving—but still annoying—way. Dawn was quieter than her older sister unless she was on the phone.

"It just means I have to work another full day myself." Claire resigned herself to the thought as she dragged her feet upstairs, barely hearing the weak "sorry" from her daughter.

In her office, a converted guest room on the second floor of their Westmount home, Claire stared at her assortment of teas. There were more than sixty of them.

"Even you seem too overwhelming right now," she said. "Another day almost over and I still don't have a single idea to save my shop. I don't know if I ever will." She dragged her feet to the bedroom.

Claire sighed and Jan gently rubbed her hand. "And now Pauline doesn't have time to help either," Claire said. "I don't know how much longer I can hold out."

Claire had opened her tea shop in 1966, a year before she and Richard began dating. The shop had been a dream she'd had to put on hold during her first marriage, but a couple of years after David's death, she had opened Claire's Tea Shop, promising herself she would never again shelve her dream for a man.

Jan had been by her side during her first marriage, had helped her open Claire's Tea Shop, and had worked occasionally in the shop as Claire juggled raising a family and running her business. Richard had helped, too, of course, but he couldn't take the children to work like Claire sometimes could. Tea shop customers cooed at the girls when they were babies, helped distract them during tantrums when Claire carried hot water across the shop, and constantly paid the girls compliments for their good behaviour. Richard would have had a hard time talking to potential home buyers while calming a temper tantrum.

Jan sipped on her all-time favourite: rose-scented Ceylon. "What about Dawn?"

"She helps, too, but she's still young. I can channel Pauline's unending energy into cleaning or unloading supply from the truck, but Dawn is always drawing—people, flowers, houses, you name it. Short of helping with ads—which I can't afford these days—she can be trying to have in the store."

Claire stared into her cup. Today it was Keemun, much easier to purchase these days now that China was trading with the West. "But with the sales as low as they are, and all I keep hearing now is how caffeine is bad for you...I feel guilty even asking Dawn to taste anything. She's thirteen. Is that too young to introduce her to caffeine?"

"I think you're over-thinking it. Besides, doesn't tea have less caffeine than coffee?"

Claire outlined the rim of her cup with her finger. "Under-thinking doesn't work either."

"Have you tried these herbal teas that have become popular?"

Claire's finger stopped and her other hand—resting on her lap—turned into a fist. "Those aren't teas. They're tisanes. This is Claire's Tea Shop, not Claire's Dried Twigs and Berries Shop."

Jan snorted and even Claire let a minuscule smile escape her attempt at a stiff upper lip.

The chimes over the front door jingled, and

Claire's heart skipped a beat as she looked up, hoping to see a customer, but it was her daughter.

"Hi, Mom." Pauline shook off her umbrella. "With all the rain, the sports rally got cancelled."

Claire had been so steeped in her own misery that she hadn't noticed the miserable weather outside. "Oh, Pauline, you're spraying that water all over!" Claire ran to the back room for a mop, which she handed to her daughter.

"Sorry." Pauline mopped up the water.

Jan nodded in approval. "Glad to see your girls help out. I hear so many stories these days about teens not helping their parents."

"I have no choice," Pauline said. "Mom's threatened to replace my wardrobe with hers if I don't."

Everyone laughed.

"Apparently, she has to wear acid-wash jeans to be cool," Claire said, her mood lifted. "Though I will never for the life of me understand what makes them cool."

Jan held up her cup. "They're cool simply because neither you nor I will wear them."

Claire raised her cup in response. "I'll drink to that!"

Pauline leaned the mop against the wall. "I came to see if you need help, but I guess not."

Claire stared at the empty store and her good mood vanished like the steam from her cup. She had updated her shop's décor several years ago so that it was still elegant but modern. Lace curtains floated over the main window, which was framed by a mauve valance and matching drapes. Rattan chairs were softened by plush cushions in mauve and pastel pink chintz. Tabletops were clear glass, supported by brass legs—something she would never buy again because the tables took forever to clean between customers. The lounge area at the back had a sophisticated, pastel pink couch with a large back and round arms, adorned with cushions that matched the chintz on the chairs. Several wicker chairs stood around the glass-and-brass coffee table.

But Claire also honoured the past. She had begun to create a wall of photos that would grow over time. Her favourite was a photo of herself and her parents at her grandparents' dining room table, with a full English afternoon tea setting in the middle. Claire was seven years old in the black-and-white photo, her hair in pigtails with curls, and wearing a white dress. Although she couldn't see her feet in the photo—the tablecloth covered them—she knew she was wearing her white patent leather shoes, shoes she was only allowed to wear on special occasions, like going to church or to Grandma and Grandpa's house for afternoon tea. Her grandparents had passed away a long time ago, and her father of a heart attack three years ago, but Claire's mother was still enjoying the high life in a luxury seniors' home in Toronto.

Claire slumped back in her chair. "I don't know what to do. I had five customers today. Three, if you only count those who bought. The other two wanted to come in and take a quick look—they had just moved to Belmont—and then they left before I even had time to offer them a whiff of tea." She cupped her chin in her hands.

Pauline took a wicker chair with no armrests, turned it around, and straddled it.

"Could you sit like a lady?" Claire said, exasperated. Somehow her proper heritage hadn't made its way to Pauline. Something must have been passed down from Richard. Clearly.

Pauline turned the chair around and sat with her legs crossed and her hands folded in her lap. "This is so uncomfortable."

"But it's proper."

Jan smiled. "I have to agree with your mom.

Sorry. But say, Pauline, do you have any ideas about how your mom can bring customers back?"

Claire had never thought to ask her daughter, and the realization embarrassed her. If she wanted one of her daughters to take over the store someday, shouldn't she ask their opinion once in a while?

"I could dress up in my mascot costume and hand out candy on Halloween when kids walk home from school," Pauline said. "When the parents ask where they got it from, the kids would say Claire's Tea Shop."

Claire shook her head. "They won't remember the store's name and would probably say they got it from a wolf. That didn't work out well for Little Red Riding Hood." Pauline's mascot costume was that of a wolf wearing her high school's jersey.

Jan slapped the table. "But what if each candy or chocolate bar or whatever had a tag attached to it that said Claire's Tea Shop on it? On the back, make a coupon. Something like 'ten percent off the next purchase of tea.' Tracy's super organized. She'd be happy to help." Tracy was Jan's daughter.

Claire thought about the idea for a moment and then shook her head. "That's a lot of toil and trouble. How many kids might come by? Twenty? Maybe thirty?"

"Not once they call their friends when they get home," Pauline said. "As long as it's not pouring rain, I can stand out there for several hours. For once, I wouldn't sweat like a pig in that costume."

Claire considered the idea a little more and then shook her head. "I don't think so, Pauline. People use tea bags because of convenience, and lots of women still smoke. That doughnut shop down the street is getting almost all my business because they offer both. A coupon won't be the long-term solution I'm looking for."

Jan patted Claire's arm. "You'll find a solution. You always do."

Pauline nodded eagerly. "I know you will, Mom."

But for a fleeting moment, Claire saw pity in her daughter's eyes. Claire's cheeks began to heat up. "I'm going for a walk. Pauline, if no one comes in the next half hour, you might as well lock up. Thanks for the pep talk, both of you, but I'm afraid the answer isn't so simple."

Claire got her coat and umbrella and headed out the back door so she wouldn't have to see that look in her daughter's eyes again.

∼

THE FOLLOWING MORNING, Richard paced back and forth behind the counter at his wife's tea shop. He'd driven to work early but had forgotten his client address book. He needed it for Halloween promo postcards. His secretary had wanted to enter it into their new computer system, but if they were stored in a computer, he worried he'd forget about them. Even just the order in which they were entered in the address book told him who his first clients were and who his latest ones were. What computer system would do that at a glance?

But when he had called home to ask Claire to bring his address book to the shop to save him a little time, Dawn had said her mom had left thirty minutes before. Richard had gone home to get his address book himself. As he drove back to his office, however, he noticed that the sign on the door still read "closed." He had to try several keys before he remembered which one opened the store.

Now he drummed his fingers on the countertop. Should he call Jan? He didn't want to needlessly worry people, but he and Claire always told each other where they'd be, and now she'd disappeared.

"I'll wait ten more minutes," he said to himself, "and then I'll call."

This year had been rough on Claire, but she

wouldn't accept any money from his salary for her store. He'd even pitched it as a loan, and she said she'd borrow from the bank if absolutely necessary.

That comment had stung.

Richard loved Claire for her dreams. He brushed his hand over the counter as he remembered how Claire had charmed him with her descriptions of tea twenty years before. He had never drunk tea before meeting Claire, but the way she described black teas with "notes" of apricot or sunshine changed his perspective on the world. Yes, it had been that profound. He didn't believe a cup of black tea could taste so beautiful, that taste and sight could sometimes cross their obvious boundaries, but he quickly learned to include similar descriptions when he sold homes.

"The neighbourhood imparts notes of roses and lilacs, especially because of Mrs. So-and-So's house down the street," he would say. Or: "You'll catch a note of apple in this home, because Mrs. So-and-So is renowned locally for her apple pie, which she bakes from premium apples. She's selling her house because she and her husband have decided to move to something smaller and open a café."

His clients' eyes lit up when he described homes like that. "Notes" meant success. The tiny hints pointed to something extraordinary, and Claire's Tea Shop was filled with extraordinary notes and run by an extraordinary woman.

Richard wouldn't be himself without Claire, but he worried that Claire wouldn't be Claire without her tea shop.

"Wait," he said to himself. "Would our marriage still be safe if the shop closed?" One worry after another flew into his mind and he stared at the wall of teas, trying to figure out which tea Claire would suggest for him in this moment. "Every feeling, problem, and celebration has a tea, doesn't it, sweetheart?" he said out loud.

The door chimes rang, jolting Richard out of his thoughts. It was her. He gasped and rushed around the counter to hug his wife.

"Where have you been? You were supposed to open an hour ago."

Claire only politely hugged him back.

Was their marriage safe?

"I went for a walk. Why did you open up?"

That she was angry at him for helping wasn't out of the ordinary. It was her store as she had told him many times. But that she didn't mind arriving this late? That wasn't like his wife. This new Claire concerned Richard more with each passing day.

"But honey, you can't expect people to come if they don't know when you're actually open."

Claire walked around the counter to the back room. "Did anyone come in?" she called through the store.

Richard stared at the floor. He had to be honest, but he didn't like the answer. "No."

Claire re-emerged. "Then there was no point in wasting your time standing there. I had the store cleaned up by the time Jan came to visit yesterday, and Pauline said no one else showed up after I left. Why waste the time?"

The tone in her voice said to leave things alone. After twenty years, Richard knew when to back down and when to nudge.

Today she might need a push, he thought. He'd watched Claire juggle motherhood, deal with her father's death, and run her business without ever becoming this depressed.

"Claire, you're my Darjeeling. It breaks my heart to see you like this."

Claire's face relaxed and the corners of her mouth turned up slightly. "And you're my Keemun."

They'd given each other these nicknames shortly after their first, sumptuous kiss.

Richard hugged her again, and this time, Claire's

embrace showed more affection. "I know you're running out of steam," he said.

"No pun intended?" Claire's smile was now the gentle, toying one he loved.

Richard smiled back. Maybe he wouldn't have to push after all. "I'm worried about you. You've always insisted on opening up on time because that's one more opportunity for someone to discover your store and come in. I mean, have you asked customers for ideas? For feedback? That's the new management technique these days. Asking for feedback."

Claire dropped into a chair. "I've done all that, and the answers are still the same: they either want to smoke inside but drink herbal teas to improve their health, or they like the convenience of tea bags."

Richard sat down opposite her and cupped her hand in his. "You've always changed with the times. Have you considered listening to your customers? Maybe it's time to offer tea bags. You could even try selling Earl Claire in tea bags. Otherwise, you'll lose the store, and…quite frankly, I'm scared I'll lose you, too."

Claire pulled her hand away and a lump formed in Richard's throat. "Absolutely not.

This is Claire's Tea Shop, not Claire's Tea Bag Shop."

Richard sat up straight and adjusted his tie. "I just see how down you are." *And cold to me*, he wanted to add but knew that would only make things worse for himself.

Claire stood up and her entire demeanour became agitated as she paced the floor, her hands emphasizing her frustration. "You don't understand! It's not just about pride, Richard, and not even just about the girls' health. About a month after I banned smoking inside the shop, I could taste and smell more. I didn't realize how much this second-hand smoke they keep talking about affected my ability to enjoy tea. I want that for my customers, too." Richard nodded and Claire continued. "The problem with tea bags is that they release all the flavour—even the bitterness—all at once. That's why they taste so bad."

"You said they do it for convenience, not taste," Richard interjected. "Isn't it time you listen to that feedback?"

His wife's response made him wish he'd said nothing.

Claire's voice become louder. "Convenience? Yeah, right. People go through all the effort to brew a pot of coffee in the morning, but they won't do that for tea? Please! Either way you need a pot, a mug, and either a filter or strainer. Fine, you need a kettle for tea, but it sits on the stove and doesn't take up counter space like a coffeemaker. What's the big difference?"

Her glare frightened Richard. He couldn't remember when he had last seen her this angry.

Claire didn't wait for a response. "When you drink loose-leaf tea, you can control the flavour. That's why I won't offer tea bags: they may be convenient but they lack personality. They're boring. They taste as industrial as the process that made them. Look at this shop, Richard!"

Richard glanced around, though he didn't know what Claire wanted him to notice.

"This place is me. There's nothing industrial about it. This shop is full of personality, *my* personality. I will not be pushed back into being a silent woman again."

Richard knew Claire was referring to her first marriage, but she rarely discussed it, and he always assumed it best not to ask. "But sweetheart, I'm not trying to make you silent. I just see what's happening—"

Claire's lips formed a tight line, and she crossed

her arms. "Then there's nothing further for you to say. I'll figure this out on my own." She stormed off to the back room.

Richard raked his hands through his hair. His wife wasn't just defending her pride—though that was part of it—she was defending her existence. He wanted to see the light in her eyes when she talked about tea again, to feel the touch of her hand on his cheek before they kissed. What else could he do to show her he truly loved her and wanted what was best? He didn't bother retrieving his coat from the back room. Handling the cold fall weather was easier than facing Claire's boiling temper again.

PAULINE PEEKED into the family room. "Anything I can get you, Mom?"

Claire, wrapped up in an afghan in her papasan chair, shook her head.

"But that's the fifth cup of Earl Claire—?"

"I'm fine," Claire snapped, her eyes fixated on the television, waiting for *Cheers* to start. Nothing good was showing on their twenty-eight channels, so she chose to watch the last episode again. Thank goodness for VCRs.

Pauline raised her hands, giving up. "Whatever, Mom. I'm going to work out."

Richard had the audacity to suggest tea bags in her shop? After twenty years, how did he not understand?

She sighed. But he was also right: Claire did work hard at keeping up with the present. She could never figure out why people stuck to useless traditions. But tea's loose-leaf tradition was easily four hundred years old. It was absolutely still useful.

Tea was as much about memories as flavour, something she didn't realize until she'd spent an hour calming down in her back room after her fight with Richard.

Sunday teatime at Grandma and Grandpa's house filled many of Claire's childhood memories. Grandma would bake crumpets and scones the way her grandmother had back in England, and everyone would use their best manners. Afternoon teatime was when Claire had learned the art of socializing. Then, once Claire had turned sixteen, her mother had allowed her to join her ladies' circles, and Claire had fit in perfectly.

Now *Cheers* began and Claire's focus oscillated between the sitcom and her memories, from Sam as he tended his bar to the women in her family serving tea.

"That's it!" she cried.

She gulped down the rest of her tea and jumped up from her seat, the afghan dropping to the floor, ideas flooding her brain and threatening to evaporate.

She rushed to her home office, slammed the door shut—out of excitement, not anger—and scrambled to scribble down her ideas. Her heart pounded: she didn't want to lose a single thought. After half an hour, her brain absolutely empty and hand cramping, she lay her pen down.

"But any idea is only good if you can afford it," she said to herself. "Can you afford this one?"

She pulled out her ledger, took a deep breath, and opened the black book. Her heart sank: if she wanted to pay next month's rent, she had to take funds from her advertising budget, which meant she couldn't advertise her idea. She certainly wasn't going to grovel to the landlord—a family friend now—and ask for a deferral on her rent. Besides, Claire refused to owe money to family or friends. Banks, fine. That was their job, though they'd already refused her a loan this year because of her slowing income. But she wouldn't ask family or friends.

Claire's idea was outside her budget.

She snapped her fingers and picked up the office phone to dial Jan. "You can do this, Claire." If anyone could help her out, it was her best friend. "She at least understands what's important to me."

A GIANT WOLF ran through the front door at Claire's Tea Shop and jumped over the counter, landing squarely on both feet.

"Pauline!" Claire scolded her costumed daughter.

Pauline's voice was muffled as she spoke. "You're the one who paid for gymnastics lessons. Be glad I grew so tall, otherwise you'd be worried sick about me on the unevens instead!" She hugged Claire tightly, and Claire had to admit her daughter was right. Watching Pauline do gymnastic stunts at such a height always brought Claire's stomach to her throat. But when the coach awkwardly told Claire that Pauline—who had reached six feet—was too tall for competitive gymnastics, Claire was secretly relieved, believing Pauline's days of stunts were over.

She had been wrong but she was still very proud

of her daughter.

Pauline stepped back and removed the wolf head. Her cheeks were rosy and her bangs were matted to her face. "I handed everything out! All two hundred bags! Your idea was a hit!"

Claire breathed a sigh of relief. She and Jan, who ran the hair salon in Belmont Village, had asked the other store owners if they would participate in a giveaway. Each bag contained candy and coupons, and read, "Happy Halloween from the Shopkeepers at Belmont Village!"

To make sure kids didn't eat the candy and then discard the bag, Pauline had handed out bags to workers exiting from their shift at the nearby factory. Once she'd handed out what she could, she walked back to Belmont Village, continuing to hand out packages as she passed people. Claire had given away another fifty packages to kids and adults who passed the store.

"I couldn't have done it without yours or Jan's help," Claire said. "I only hope those coupons bring more business to all the shopkeepers." The thought made Claire nervous, because a lack of sales on their part might undermine her reputation, which was excellent. But she didn't beg, and she didn't borrow any money. She only offered a service.

Pauline set her wolf head on the desk in the back room, removed her wolf paws, and reached into the fridge for the sandwiches her mom kept there.

"Wouldn't you rather eat at home?" Claire asked.

A tuna sandwich already unwrapped, Pauline answered, "Nope. But you need to get home. Jan's waiting for you to do your hair." She took a bite.

"What?" Did Claire have an appointment she'd forgotten about? No, wait. Pauline had said Jan was at their house. To do her hair?

"Just go home, put on your best Claire's Tea Shop outfit, and Jan will do your hair. Then come back here in two hours."

"Why?"

"There's going to be a party." Pauline placed the sandwich on the wrapper on the desk and stood up. "Now get going." She gently pushed her mother toward the front door.

"What party?"

"You'll see. Now go!"

Claire could just barely grab her purse as the half-wolf/half-daughter continued leading her mother to the front door.

Claire laughed. "All right, all right! But this had better be good, Pauline. You know I—"

"Don't like working late," Pauline finished. "I know. This isn't work. Mostly. Just go!"

Claire took one look back at her daughter as she closed the front door behind her and caught Pauline looking at the clock that hung over the doorway to the back room. She was clearly waiting for something, but what or who? What was this all about?

RICHARD STUCK his head in the back door. "Is she gone?" he whispered to Pauline.

Pauline nodded.

Richard entered carrying a full garbage bag, followed by Dawn, her camera bag slung over her shoulder. He handed Pauline the bag. "Do I have to?"

Pauline and Dawn giggled as they pulled items out of it. Dawn set a travel sewing kit on the desk.

"After trying to convince Mom she should sell tea bags, Dad, *especially* of Earl Claire, you owe her," Dawn replied. "You tackle that side, Pauline, and I'll start here."

Both girls immediately set down to sew. A knock

at the back door startled Richard, but he breathed a sigh of relief when it wasn't Claire. Not that she would knock, but her arriving early would have ruined the surprise. He invited in the owners of the Belmont Village flower shop. "I may not know how to help your mother with her store," he said to his daughters, "but if there's one thing I do know, it's how to decorate with flowers. Makes any home five grand more expensive."

The girls laughed and Richard helped carry in small vases filled with Halloween-themed bouquets. He began re-arranging tables. The less time he spent in the vicinity of the girls and their sewing project, the better it would be for his pride.

Richard only had two hours to transform Claire's Tea Shop into a Halloween party that still exuded his wife's elegant, modern, inviting, and friendly personality. Two weeks ago, he had overheard Claire on the phone talking to Jan. Her voice had been unusually ecstatic so his curiosity had gotten the better of him and he had kept listening. The more Claire had explained her ideas to Jan, the more ideas Richard had.

And they didn't involve tea bags.

He talked with Jan the next day, who talked with her daughter while Richard spoke with his two. Their plans to help were set within twenty-four hours.

Now as he arranged the flowers on the tables, he did worry about one thing: the florists had tried their best to find Halloween-coloured flowers with a weak scent, but Richard could still detect their aroma. Would Claire object?

"Halloween with floral notes." He smiled. If he knew his wife as well as he hoped he did, she'd make a new tea blend with that scent.

"You still won't tell me what this is all about, will you?" Claire asked Jan as she admired herself in the mirror. "Pauline said to come dressed for the shop. I always do."

Jan wrapped the cord around her now-cooled curling iron and set it in her bag. "To be honest, Claire, lately you haven't. You've let yourself go a little."

The longer Claire stared at her reflection, the more she realized she needed to acknowledge the truth. Jan was an incredible hairstylist, and she could give Claire's brown locks more body and sway than Claire could herself. Because Jan had taught

Claire over the years how to style her hair, Claire always left the house looking elegant and fashionable.

But maybe not lately.

"I guess you're right. It's hard when the numbers at the shop aren't good. My net profit this month will be twenty dollars if I'm lucky." She fluffed the ruffle down the front of her blouse and tugged at the puffy shoulders. She looked at Jan in the mirror. "Do you think my idea will turn things around?"

Jan's eyes brightened. "Of course it will. It's too good not to. Now it's time to go!"

"Even if you won't tell me what the party is about," Claire said with a laugh.

The women grabbed their purses and headed to the foyer. Jan slipped into her coat, but Claire threw hers over her arm so she wouldn't ruin the shoulders on her blouse.

"You know what? I am so lucky to have you as a friend, Jan." Claire hugged her. "Thank you for standing by me. Whatever happens, I hope we'll always be friends."

Jan hugged Claire back. "Always. I promise. Cross my heart and hope to die, buried with tea bags."

The women laughed as they stepped outside.

The last day of October could be warm or cool, and clear, rainy, or snowy. This year, Halloween weather was cool and clear, the perfect combination for a lovely evening of trick-or-treating.

"I know Pauline and I handed out all the goodie bags today, but my budget ran out to make any more. I doubt it will be enough to make a difference."

"Stop worrying about the future. Enjoy the scenery. Look—the Hogans have the best decorations out this year, don't you think?" Jan pointed to a house decked out in Halloween paraphernalia.

Although Claire hadn't lived in Westmount—the neighbourhood to the west of Belmont Village—when she'd first opened Claire's Tea Shop, she lived there now. She loved the fifteen-minute walk past houses designed by different architects, mature trees that added to the elegance of the neighbourhood, and the seasonal decorations before every holiday. As she and Jan walked to the store, seeing the jack-o-lanterns lit from the inside with candles lifted her spirits.

But the walk did nothing to calm her nerves. Once they reached the corner of Claremont and Belmont, Claire stopped and grabbed Jan by the shoulder. "You have to tell me what's going on. I can't handle the suspense!"

But Jan only grinned.

"Fine, be that way."

Then they rounded the corner. Claire gasped. A group of ten or fifteen people, mostly women, stood outside her store.

"Who are they?"

Jan shrugged. "I have no idea."

"You know very well—"

"Nope, no clue. With Tracy's help, we slipped an official invitation for a Halloween tea tasting into your goodie bags."

Claire's heart jumped. Tea tasting? On Halloween? These strangers had decided to come here tonight instead of handing out treats from their doorsteps?

"We played on the ideas you told me about and came up with 'trick or tea.'"

"Well, I've certainly been tricked!" Claire kissed Jan on the cheek. "But thank you!"

At the door, a fox mascot wearing a toque and parka that said 'Kitchener Blizzard' handed her a rose. Next to the local hockey team's mascot stood a big wolf—Pauline—also handing out flowers.

Jan leaned over and whispered, "Richard knows the fox's mom."

The fox bowed courteously while the wolf playfully urged everyone to step aside and allow Claire space as though she were royalty. Pauline opened the door and Claire entered.

She clapped her hands to her cheeks. "Richard did this, didn't he?"

Jan nodded.

Vases of elegant, small bouquets in oranges and creams adorned each table, while twisted garlands of crepe paper hung along the walls. Cardboard ghosts were taped to the display case that housed the day's baked goods and sandwiches, and a fat jack-o-lantern with a friendly, toothy grin and a candle inside sat next to the cash register.

Claire inhaled deeply. "He even chose flowers with little scent."

Jan pulled Claire by the arm to the lounge area in the back, the two stopping along the way to greet guests. Some faces she recognized, while others were complete strangers. But Claire had to blink back tears as some of her most loyal customers introduced her to their friends who had never before patronized her store.

Claire's heart was ready to burst. Her family and

best friend had organized all of this without telling her. Then she spotted her husband and doubled over in laughter.

Standing before her was a six-foot tall man, his face and arms poking out of a white sheet that had been folded in half and sewn together at the sides. A string with a tag hung from the top of his head. Pillows affixed to the inside of the sheet gave him bulk, while mud smeared along the bottom half of the sheet was clearly meant to be tea.

Claire stood up, tears streaming down her face from laughter, when Richard handed her the tag.

"Penance Herbal Tea," she read out loud. "Helps your husband say he's sorry."

She doubled over, laughing till she cried.

"The girls were aghast when they found out I'd suggested you sell tea bags," Richard confessed. "With Earl Claire in them. They sided with you one hundred percent and said I had to *bag* for forgiveness."

Claire groaned at the pun. "By dressing as my nightmare?" She dried her eyes and hoped her mascara wasn't running.

"Actually, a few people said that now that they've seen a dirty, life-sized tea bag, they might switch back to loose leaf!"

Claire tried to hug Richard, but she bounced off the bumper of pillows. Laughing again, she settled for a peck on his cheek.

"But there's still more." Richard stepped aside and gestured to three tables set up close to the wall behind him. Jan now stood at one, Dawn at the second one, and Tracy—dressed as Cyndi Lauper—stood behind the third table. Each table had small paper cups, an electric kettle, and a few tins of tea.

Claire clapped her hands. "This is the tea tasting! It looks so inviting!" Her daughter, best friend, and best friend's daughter smiled back at her.

"I overheard your conversation with Jan, and as we discussed it the next day, I realized we could take your idea one step further and start it tonight," Richard said. "So many adults want something fun for themselves on Halloween, and I thought we could invite them here for a new experience." He pointed to a father sitting off to the side with two children, the girl wearing a pink wig and pink sparkly dress, and the boy's face hidden behind a plastic action-hero mask, with a plastic action-hero costume draped over his body. "And because you've banned smoking, they're happy to bring their kids. No babysitters required."

More tears formed in Claire's eyes. "You've thought of everything, haven't you?"

Richard blushed. "Except the costume. That was all the girls' doing."

Claire snuck another peck on Richard's cheek.

A woman dressed as a witch stepped up to the tables and asked about the teas. Claire smiled as Jan, Dawn, and Tracy described their blends using the vocabulary for tea tasting she had taught them over the years. The woman sniffed each sample while they spoke. As she sipped her selection, Richard introduced Claire to the witch, who turned out to be the fox mascot's mother.

"Claire, this tea is exquisite. I'd like to buy some right now. What is it again? It's so incredible I've already forgotten."

Claire took a quick whiff and furrowed her brow. "Um, I actually don't know." She stared at Jan.

"It's called Lover's Twist," Jan said. "Your husband here tried to create a blend of his own, but I helped. Plus, I called up your mom for advice. She sends her best but didn't want to drive the 401 to get here. She said the four-lane stretch between Milton and Cambridge is horrendous."

Claire nodded. "That sounds like Mom." Claire

reached for a sample of Lover's Twist. She inhaled its aroma and took a sip. "I taste…chocolate." She took another sip. "Cinnamon. Cardamom." Then a few more. "On a smooth base of blended teas. It smells great. Thank you for doing this."

Richard leaned over and whispered. "Sounds like an aphrodisiac to me."

"That's back-room talk, Richard," Jan scolded. "I don't need to hear that."

Richard raised an eyebrow at Jan. "Doesn't my wife tell you these things, anyways?"

Jan's cheeks reddened.

Dawn plugged her ears. "But your daughter doesn't need to hear it!"

After the laughter died down, Dawn said to the witch, "We have tins ready to go. You can pay at the counter. However, we're running a special tonight —"

The witch pointed her finger. "Yes! I saw the coupon. I'd love to book a private tea party right away."

"Oh!" Tracy said with a Cyndi Lauper-esque squeal. "That's my department! I'm supposed to make sure girls just want to have fun tonight!" She picked up a pen and clipboard and took down the woman's name and number.

My first tea party customer, Claire thought, herself trying to remain professional, though she was ready to break down into tears of gratitude and relief.

Like the bar on *Cheers*, she would set up the shop with the tables in a semi-circle around a serving table, with different types of tea already portioned in small bowls so she could demonstrate the difference in leaves and flavouring techniques. She would also introduce attendees to green tea, which was gaining in popularity but not widely available in tea bags. As she spoke to other shopkeepers about her Halloween giveaway, the chocolatier suggested they could exchange products: she would sell a selection of teas that paired well with chocolate, while Claire would offer some of her specialty bars. Claire had agreed. At the end of each party, Claire would give each attendee a small tin of their favourite tea, the opportunity to buy any tea that evening for twenty percent off, a coupon valid for the next thirty days for ten percent off, and a small box of chocolates with an additional coupon for the chocolatier. Jan had helped Claire refine the idea but they couldn't figure out how to get the word out past the goodie bags.

"I thought showing people what a tea-tasting party entailed would help spread the word faster,"

Richard said. "In the end, you really only need maybe ten people who'll bring at least five with them, right? Then they can help spread the word *and* say that they'd already tried the tea. Plus, I needed a reason to touch base with my clients and I wanted the brokerage to stand out from others who just send empty 'Happy Halloween, we can sell your house' postcards."

Claire's mouth dropped. "So in addition to the goodie bags…?"

"I sent out three hundred postcards on behalf of the brokerage as part of our networking efforts. In fact, one of my colleagues suggested having you offer tea to buyers at the open houses of high-end homes. I can't believe that in the twenty years since our first date, I never thought of that."

Claire shook her head in amazement.

"And before you say anything, yes, I paid for the flowers. Since I was using your shop as a networking event for my business, it seemed only fair."

Claire snorted as she stared at his costume. "So this is how you network now? In an old sheet covered in mud?"

Richard playfully pouted and crossed his arms. "Goes to show that I have good clients—they still trust an old tea bag!" This was the woman he'd fallen in love with, and nothing made him happier than to see his wife hopeful again.

Just then, the wolf and fox entered the shop. They high-fived people as they walked through the crowd, and Dawn stepped away from her tea-tasting table to take photos of those who wanted them.

Richard stretched his arms around Claire, squishing the pillow between them. "So now that you've sipped that aphrodisiac tea…"

Claire placed her hand on his cheek. "Yes?" Her skin tingled, a sensation she hadn't felt in a long time.

Richard knew he looked ridiculous, but any woman who looked at him like his wife did right now, even when he was dressed as a life-sized tea bag, was someone deeply in love with him.

Dawn's camera flashed. At her parents' surprised look, she flashed a sheepish grin. "You looked so cute!"

A little commotion had built behind them, and Claire watched how her older daughter and the Kitchener Blizzard's fox sparred with each other as though they were at a real game. Dawn checked the number of pictures left on her film and closed in on the mascots, taking several shots. After the fox let the wolf win their little skirmish, they shook hands and removed their mascot heads.

The fox was a young man. His eyes popped out of his head when he saw Pauline's face. "You're a girl?"

Flash.

The crowd laughed.

For the first time in her life, Claire saw Pauline blush. Not out of embarrassment—she didn't look away. Instead, she looked straight at him, dipping her chin slightly.

Richard whispered, "You see that?"

Claire nodded. "My only worry is that if they do date, no staircase, chair, or couch will be safe in our home from all their gymnastics."

Richard kissed Claire on the cheek, and she turned and smiled at him. He took her hand. "How about a little more back-room talk…?"

She raised an eyebrow and replied in a sultry voice, "I think I even know a back room we could use."

She chuckled to herself as she led him away. If the first twenty years of their relationship included kissing a tea bag out of love and gratitude, what would the next twenty years bring?

ACKNOWLEDGMENTS

Books never produce themselves, so I'd like to thank the following people who helped with *Trick or Tea*.

- All Things Tea in Belmont Village. Read more about them in the following section.
- Heather Wright and Susan Fish, my editors.
- Michelle Fairbanks of Fresh Design, my graphic designer.
- Dani Baker for allowing me to use her Kitchener Blizzards from *Santa's Last Muffin*, part of her *Hansel & Pretzel* cozy mystery series. Dani's novels are set in a German bakery in Kitchener. She writes in German but has translated some of her novels into English. Visit DaniBakerBooks.com for more details.
- My mentor, Ali MacGee.

- My family for their support and memories: Mom and Dad; Corey, Khristopher, and Jonnathan; Pat and Kelly; Kristin, Mike, Xander, and Cody.
- You: Thank you for staying subscribed.

AFTERWORD

Belmont Village does indeed exist and is a wonderful, quaint shopping and eating strip on Belmont Avenue in Kitchener. *Claire's Tea Shop* takes place in 1967, whereas *Trick or Tea* takes place in 1987. Several changes happened in the intervening 20 years. For starters. Belmont Village as a name for the area came into being, and Belmont West was renamed to Belmont Avenue.

Although the stores and businesses I use in *Love on Belmont* are fictional, there may be overlap with a real store. If I feel the story might have an effect on an existing store, I speak with the owner(s) first to ensure they're comfortable with me moving forward with my idea.

For *Tea Shop for Two* (2021) and its prequels, that

store is All Things Tea, owned and run by George Broughton. I'll be honest: I never liked black tea before starting this series, so I was a bit nervous about writing a book about a tea shop. But tea and books go together like Lois Lane and Clark Kent, music and dance, winter and snow (at least where I live). I had to open *Love on Belmont* with it. So, if I was going to write about the world of tea, I had to step out of my herbal/rooibos comfort zone, and I'm so glad I did. George has been extremely supportive in helping me learn about the world of tea. I still love Keemun, but I'm very surprised that, depending on the day, my palette wants Ceylon or Darjeeling, because it can actually taste the difference.

STAY IN TOUCH

Did you enjoy the book? You can stay in touch with Lori by visiting LoveOnBelmont.com and signing up for Lori's newsletter. She writes each one herself, so it's her words to you. You'll receive updates on *Love on Belmont* and other books, be the first to hear about specials, and get deleted scenes. Plus, if you haven't read the short story prequels to *Tea Shop for Two*, you can download them for free by subscribing.

ENJOY ALL THE LOVE ON BELMONT BOOKS

Join Claire, Richard and all your other friends on Belmont Avenue, where love and tea create a magical blend 🤍.

THE LOVE ON BELMONT PREQUEL SHORT STORIES

1. Claire's Tea Shop
2. Trick or Tea
3. Oh, Christmas Tea

THE LOVE ON BELMONT NOVELS

1. Tea Shop for Two
2. Oh, What the Fudge
3. Teas of Joy

Visit LoveOnBelmont.com to buy your next book!

ABOUT LORI

Lori's first memory of the Belmont neighbourhood is of her falling out of her bed at her grandparents' home when she was perhaps three. Opa, her grandfather, sadly passed away in his mid-60s, but that didn't stop Oma, her grandmother, from creating many, many happy memories in her home for her family.

Across the tracks and up a set of cement stairs was Belmont Village, a quaint shopping strip. Oma always bought her lottery tickets there and often took Lori and her sister to the convenience store to buy them a sugary treat. Mom took them, too, sometimes.

But at the time, Lori had no idea Belmont neighbourhood and Belmont Village would be the source of the most wonderful romance in her life: her future husband.

When she met her future in-laws about 20 years later, they learned they had already met: Lori's in-laws had run that small convenience store until the mid-80s. Moreover, their paths had crossed often with those of Lori's mom's family before Lori was even a thought.

Happy memories, shared fates, love…

And shopping.

How could Belmont Village *not* be the perfect place to set a sweet romance series about different couples in different stages of a relationship?

Lori lives in Waterloo, Ontario, with her husband and two sons and visits Belmont Village whenever she can.

- facebook.com/loriwolfheffner
- x.com/LoriWolfHeffner
- instagram.com/loriwolfheffner
- goodreads.com/lori_wolf-heffner
- bookbub.com/author/lori-wolf-heffner
- pinterest.com/loriwolfheffner
- amazon.com/author/loriwolfheffner

www.ingramcontent.com/pod-product-compliance
Lightning Source LLC
Chambersburg PA
CBHW060412080526
44583CB00012B/546